Blood, Metal, Fiber, Rock

Blood, Metal, Fiber, Rock

Poems by

Elizabeth Bodien

Kelsay Books

Cover Art: *Basket #71*
Phyllis Dunning, Gabriola, British Columbia, Canada.

ISBN: 13-978-1-947465-37-4

Kelsay Books
Aldrich Press
www.kelsaybooks.

~~~~~~~~~~~~~~~~~~~~~~~~~~~~~~

A music broke out / and walked in the swirling snow / with long steps. / Everything on the way towards the note C. / A trembling compass directed at C. / One hour higher than the torments. / It was easy! / Behind turned-up collars everyone was smiling.

<div align="right">from "C Major" by Tomas Tranströmer</div>

~~~

When our tears are dry on the shore / and the fishermen carry their nets home / and the seagulls return to bird island / and the laughter of children recedes at night, there shall still linger the communion we forged / the feast of oneness whose ritual we partook of....It cannot be the music we heard that night / that still lingers in the chambers of memory. / It is the new chorus of our forgotten comrades / and the halleluyahs of our second selves.

from "Rediscovery" by Kofi Awoonor

~~~

Dry bones! Dry bones! I find my loving heart, / Illumination brought to such a pitch / I see the rubblestones begin to stretch / As if reality had split apart / And the whole motion of the soul lay bare: / I find that love, and I am everywhere.

<div align="right">from "The Renewal" by Theodore Roethke</div>

Acknowledgments

Thanks to the following publishers where these poems, some in slightly different versions, have appeared.

Apiary (The Hive): "As Women Sang, Crickets Would Pause"

Artemis: "After Hearing Sylvia Plath Read 'Tulips'"

Avocet: "The Blues of Sky"

Cimarron Review: "Again, Deer Season"

Connecticut River Review: "Plaid"

Contemporary Ghazals: "Lodestar" and "Of Gods"

Contemporary Haibun Online: "Jazz"

Crannóg (Ireland): "How to Be an Enigma"

Deep Water Literary Journal (Cork, Ireland): "All Souls' Night"

East Coast Literary Review: "The Twelfth Hour"

The Fourth River: "Evelyn Snake Woman"

Layers of Language: "Hwyl"

Lehigh Valley Vanguard: "Red Wind," "Remains"

Oberon: "Evensong"

Parabola: "Ewer," "The Endless Climb," "Perfect Pitch,"
    "Solace"

Pennessence: "Ebb Tide"

Philadelphia Poets: "You Are My River"

Poetry Ink: "Baroque Con Brio," "Gui: The Chinese Character for
    Tortoise," "War," "Watching the Daytona 500," and "When the
    Women Return"

Poets for Living Waters (online): "Missa Brevis Pro Oceano"

Rathalla Review: "Roar of the Girl in the Room"

Schuylkill Valley Journal: "Ocean Fabric"

Snapdragon – The Art of Creating Issue: "Two Voices"

U.S. 1 Worksheets: "Moody Window," "Blue Boy," "Aqua Glass," "Torso," "Two Pages Together," and "Violet Edges*"*

Write Here, Write Now: Greater Lehigh Valley Writers Group Anthology: "Advances"

You Are Here: The Journal of Creative Geography, The Translation Issue, in the essay "Code-Switching a Poem": "After Hearing Sylvia Plath Read 'Tulips'"

"The Rubble Women" was previously published in *Endpapers* Finishing Line Press, 2011.

"A Humble Shift of Mind," and "Sequins" were both previously published in *I Sing the Undersung*, Local Gems Press, 2017.

"Blood, Metal, Fiber, Rock" was a Semi-Finalist for the 2017 Fish Poetry Prize (Ireland), Jo Shapcott, Judge.

"In That Garden" and "Moon Flight" were Finalists in the *Atlanta Review* International Poetry Competition in March 2016.

"Mala Aria" was a Semi-Finalist for the 2013 Fish Poetry Prize, (Ireland), Paul Durcan, Judge.

Contents

Blood, Metal, Fiber, Rock

I. Blood

II. Metal

III. Fiber

IV. Rock

Notes

About the Author

Blood, Metal, Fiber, Rock

First
the shaman
dips a bended finger
into sticky blood of eland,
draws the beast up on the cave.
The creature lopes off into cracks -
those sometime doors to spirit worlds.
The shaman lays both hands upon the wall
and women come to drum the healing rhythms.
With these hands that draw and drum and touch,
four scattered worlds are moved to speak as one,
and so made whole.

See
that noble shield
formed for Achilles
by Hephaestus, god of fire.
Depicting peace, and forged to keep
the man who'd wield its weight in war,
hub to rim, the shield's constructed well
with silver, bronze, expensive gold, and tin.
The shield won't last, nor will its fated bearer.
It dares to encompass the whole known earth —
the august cities, landscapes drawn so grand,
we stand in awe.

Come and witness
mortal maid and goddess, weavers who compete
to see who of the boasting two can best create
one single dazzling tapestry of storied art.
They hitch up skirts and thread the warps.
First Pallas weaves scenes of the gods —
four color schemes to win the prize.
Proud Arachne bests the goddess,
stirs the ire that churns the girl
into a spider who can't stop
her weaving silver
webs of hope.

All commences
at the crossing, calm pinpoint before creation.
Monks blow crushed rock through slender tubes
to make designs of yellow ochre, ornate white,
bright gypsum blue, and sandstone's red.
The complex worlds of gods and humans
emerge in time from hands of many
monks who study and understand
that once created, this mandala,
like the cosmos it portrays,
will run a rocky course
and end.

I. Blood

At the Circumference

fast approaching
the day of reckoning
as the sun rises
screeching owls take flight
we stand with mouths gaping

we have forgotten
the rules of engagement
when the clock strikes
there is barely listening
the slow moan of the pith

the storybook stork
who carried so many
now balks and flies
from abetting more births
the imbalance of species

all right, go ahead
sing of what cheers you
like a disease
let us, the despairing
catch your insipid tune

as for me
I imagine great shafts of light
angels riding them down
to carry the fervent
towards a Blake sort of bliss

you, the invisible
how would you appear
moved and moving
if we only could see
your sound and your taste

In That Garden

The well-wrought story – Adam and his Eve –
so lush, so fraught, what are we to believe?
The elements are plain and yet a riddle.
It all depends on what lies in the middle
and who's at fault and who's the one to pardon
among the players in that famous garden.

Most depictions of the primal garden
show central figures – Adam, his mate Eve –
who do the deeds that lead to the need for pardon.
They want so much to know and to believe,
they eat of the banned tree that stands at the middle
because its fruit is said to solve the riddle.

What's good, what's bad – the tree's enticing riddle –
were answers for the finding in that garden?
Take note how paintings put the tree at the middle
with serpent coiling round it, tempting Eve.
And why is she so willing to believe?
She's innocent, knows no such word as "pardon."

One must partake of evil to seek pardon.
Before the apple, is there any riddle?
And how's that serpent able to believe,

to be informed of flora in that garden?
Because arriving first before our Eve?
Maybe the wily serpent's at the middle.

Suppose instead the fruit lies at the middle –
that apple hinting penalty or pardon.
The luscious need to know so tempted Eve.
Would we not also wish to learn the riddle
from sweet, forbidden fruit in that same garden,
to start (or finish) what we might believe?

Then Adam's next, when he's asked to believe.
The story puts him briefly at the middle
until the final player of the garden,
the one we hope will exercise a pardon.
Instead he penalizes. That's the riddle.
No hope for tree, for serpent, Adam, Eve.

If "Eve" means "the living," as linguists believe,
the riddle places us at the story's middle –
still asking pardon…while we waste the garden.

Of Gods

Which god would take us under watchful care
if we petitioned so in gentle prayer?

Who makes the river sing so bright at dawn
and hum at dusk an elemental prayer?

What goddess draped in blue diaphanous gown
enchants the moon with sentimental prayer?

My child at bedside whispers simple words,
her artless wish a monumental prayer.

If gods abound, too many to pay heed,
are we amiss with detrimental prayer?

And I, as some have asked before,
ask, What if *all* is accidental prayer?

At the Brink

when the unquiet dead walk down by the sea
wailing, rejoicing as if alive,
you may be curious

you may want to listen
I cannot say, stop, but do take precautions
– and also this:

carry a cable to hold very tight
to pull yourself back to the living
from there

for their voices enchant with sticky fragrance
not of sure wisdom, they also seek
who they are

some may address you, eager to show off
fancy fandangles, while others may shun
your jagged edges

the veil is not heavy but holds its sway
until your time to enter the timeless
before then you will write

for now your teardrops, scent of white tulips,
and humble prayer are offering enough
at that shore

Missa Brevis Pro Oceano

Kyrie eleison, have mercy upon us,
we the gluttons, the arrogant species.
Ocean, I cry for you,
my tears so small, your waters immense.
Is it true that you weep,
that you wail as you suffocate?
Billions of creatures live in your depths,
are they gasping now as blackness descends,
as deadly blankets drift down towards your bed?
Life forms scuttle and shake, no way to escape.
Sharks, confused, turn circles in terror.
Gulls, sticky with sludge, flail their weak feathers.

Gloria! Gloria! Oh, glorious world –
this lustrous, this wondrous, this blue-green spinning planet!
Ocean, we're sorry.
How did we come to this?
How did things go so very wrong?
Is the damage we've done forever and ever?

Qui tollis peccata mundi, miserere nobis.
You who take away the sins of the world, have mercy upon us.
Plankton, we're sorry.
Let currents carry you far from the scourge.
Nekton, we're sorry.

Swim, if you can, away to safe water.
Neuston, forgive us, your death at our hands.
Before long, your death will be our death, too.

Suscipe deprecationem nostrum.
Hear now our prayer.
Benthos, we beg you,
who live in dark seabeds,
you who devour what sinks down from above,
please help us now.

Sanctus, sanctus. Holy, holy, your waters.
Sanctus, sanctus. Waters teeming with life.
Holy the circlefish, spidercrab, giant kelp.
Holy the loggerhead turtle, the pelican.
Holy the osprey, the orca, and octopus.
Holy sea cucumbers, barnacles, starfish.

Holy the stilts, and lobsters, and urchins.
Holy the blue-footed booby, the clams.
Holy the seals, sea fans, and sharks.
Holy egret, potfish, spotted bumblebee shrimp.
Oh holy sailfish, sturgeon, and shad.
Holy the zebra worms, flatworms, and prawns.
Holy the humpbacks, dolphins, and squid.
Holy the coral, krill, crabs and cormorants.

Holy the herons, the geese, and the gulls.
Holy the driftfish, bonefish, and ballyhoo.
Holy mullet, monkfish, marlin, and tuna.
Holy holy all life who make water their home.

Benedictus, benedictus. Blessed are those
who are meek, who make peace.
Ocean, I cry for you,
my tears so small, your waters immense.
Is it true that you sigh
as your life forms all suffocate?

How will it end?
Will the peace be alive or the peace of the dead?
My prayer joins the others.
Dona nobis pacem in oceanus.
Dona nobis pacem in terra.
Please give us peace in ocean, on earth.

Ocean Fabric

Tectonic plates – basaltic cloth –
rip, divide, and wrench apart.
Torn, the ocean's bed of rock
spews up white sulfuric gasses.

Purple-deep, the crust erupts,
spitting hot, acidic water.
Flaming magma bubbles up,
hisses, cools to lava pillows.

Larger creatures shun these seams.
Blooms of tiny microbes thrive,
skirt the fissures, fringe the vents
where undersea volcanoes burst.

Plaids of ribbon worms and scaleworms,
tubeworms cluster like chenille.
Tight brocades of barnacles
and eyeless shrimp fold into darkness.

Chain-stitched mountains run the bias,
a ridge-and-canyon corduroy.
Mantle buckles, sends up minerals,
chemicals, the stuff of life.

Earth creates itself in mayhem,
fashions styled in fire-and-brimstone.
No subtle silks, no stable satins,
ocean's cloth is seismic flux.

Hwyl

Into the all of it, hint of a breeze
born of nothing and wishes
skims the surface of the dark seas

stirring up silvers of fishes,
breathes sweet whispers into the world
spinning in spirals and hisses,

plays the waves, curled and uncurled,
making fun, taking risks, stretching soul,
learning the elements, lessons like pearls

catching big gusts in a bowl,
swilling and swelling swift to full sail
skirting the shallows, the shoals

drawing in wisdom and giving it wail,
telling of wonder and weep,
crescendo of message, the squall and the gale

blowing hard, roaring loud, going deep,
shadows and sorrows churning, subsiding,
exhausted and falling towards sleep

pillows and secrets, the deep ones abiding,
words hushing to quiet again
breath   slowing   slowing   to dying
for now, back to nothing.   Amen.

Under a Gauzy Moon

From black icy waters, limpid and sleek,
she rises to tell of furtive worlds beneath.
Up from my bed, I tremble to meet her,
old as I am and still without answers.

She slinks, evades, watching me sideways,
sounding and testing whether I'm worthy.
Her movements beguile with shillowing music,
her twists and her twinings, her muscular hum.

She is my waking, my drink, and my dreadful.
Did I call her up from my fierce, fitful sleep?
She holds the moon with fiery blue eyes
blowing a fey, changing wind here before me.

I feel my blood race towards a sucking abyss.
If I say yes to her, what must I do?
She squalls in cascades at my pitiful cowardice,
"Risk always resides where the sea is unswum."

Here, then, the stand-off: I slip on wishwash,
sink to the depths of bland indecision.
From furrowed fins, pockmarked and dusky,
she draws a wing feather of dead albatross.

Puzzled, I stare. The thing has its own light.
My arms reach out for this undeserved gift.
"This quill is for you, perhaps but remembrance,
unless you decide to take it in hand."

I hold the quill, notice it shimmer,
look up to find she has vanished from view.
All that remains – ever-widening ripples
that swell, close back in, and softly engulf.

Aqua Glass

I meander these alleys, gravity of stone.
I stare as they pass. No, I know no one.
Yellow cadmium houses, the day hot on bare arms.
I duck lines of clothing. What am I searching?

A sandal maker's window opens to street.
A boy sits smoothing leather, humming a tune.
I slip into an archway, cool respite from sun.
Why did I come here? How did I arrive?

I step out to street, climb from cobbles to grass,
past the amphitheater, its long tacit tiers.
Under silver of olive trees, I turn and sit,
look over the village, out to the ocean.

I squint and it's glass – ochre and aqua,
jumble of houses, marble of water,
blood-red of roof, doors painted blue,
and ever, forever, the cerulean sea.

I lived here before. Yes, I lived here before.
I was a man with a wife and a son.
Where are they now? What is my name?
I lean into the land to tell me the story.

On a Bridge from Nowhere to Nowhere

Yes, I remember –
the night of the blizzard
behind the dark house,
we left the grown-ups,
pushed the thick wooden door
to close heavy behind us.

We trudged the vanishing
indentation of walkway
through snow-blanketed evergreens
to that far ghostly bridge,
a barely visible structure
in the great snowy void.

At last on the bridge,
our boots heavy with snow,
we stood still as statues
in a blessing of white,
as we felt the warmth
of our embrace.

The two of us kissed,
one single kiss,
ambrosia kiss
that granted a sweetness,
once and forever,
in that marble oblivion.

Innocence

Do you want a life unlived?
Take the seashell. Put it down,
before you see its ridges, shadows.
Take the sand beneath your feet –
don't let it get into your shoe.
Take the clouds, but do not name them.
Take this pencil. Guilty, too.
Weather vane that spins the wind,
does any arrow point to true?
You smell supper? Are you hungry?
Appetites aren't innocent.
Divide or bring the boats together,
watch them breathe the ocean's swell.
Who wants pure? Seaweed is messy.
So is jazz, and Irish stew.

The Blues of Sky

The sky presents a turquoise blue
of childhood summers, screen-door friends
above the darkening line of trees
crowding the highway at day's end.

Beyond long stretches overhead
of wires slack from pole to pole,
that tone of sky rings electric blue
– sheeny metal, hardware cold.

And there at the horizon's fold
where a storm has come undone,
that blue is gray with hint of rose,
last farewell from sinking sun.

But Moon, the hue near you has won.
Your alabaster whites offset
so royal blue a satin sky
that I would lie across your bed.

It all depends on what's nearby.
Different angles of the view
make myriad blues of evening sky,
the circumstantial moods of you.

Jazz

Boy and girl, giddy in love, arms linked, barely notice the traffic
light as they wait to cross the street. The spring evening is young.
They lean into it, into each other. The light changes, traffic stops.
They trip from the curb, step, turn, and glide to the other side.

> two nimble bodies
> play the black and white crosswalk
> lifting music

You, Me, and the Trout

i.   Allegro vivace

The water ripples, vowels spilling fast.
Look! flash of fish, scales sparkling, swish of fin,
arpeggios in the current running past –
all this when you but knock to enter in.
I open. There you stand and, in that minute,
we smile, stunned by delight, and welcome in it.

At last I say, come in. Each plays the part.
Please have a seat. You do. Now what comes next?
We're new at this but eager so to start.
Each tries to conjure up the fitting text.
We laugh. It doesn't matter if we miss.
We're thrilled. We realize both are feeling this.

I go for drinks – such sweet vertigo.
We are dizzy, high from just our meeting.
We sit, talk long, sink to adagio,
each effervescent glance a novel greeting.
The evening hours touch lightly as they fly
until the dogged hour of goodbye.

ii. Andante

So this is how love grows – delicious, slow.
Lax muscles, lazy fish in mid-day sun.
I take a breath and draw across my bow.
The strings stretch out, then spring to start a run.
Quick flip of tail, enough to start a glide,
we swim in luscious melodies inside.

You Are My River

My love, my flivver of beautiful,
warm is the sun, your eye-sparkle ripples.
I swim in you, River, slosh in your streams.

Your currents enfold me,
holding, caressing,
down floating down,
rolling me over.

Rest quick on your boulders,
your gray rumble bones,
shoulders and corners.
I slip into shallows,
surfacing, swishing.

Whirlpool your waist,
eddies wailing and whirling.
Swivel me, River,
all bellow and yell,
trembling the fingers,
fritling the toes.

Rise up, dive deeper,
            we're met and we're swallow
     luscious the liquid

trilling the thighs.

Here the shrill highest notes,
                    here sumptuous skins

    blood crashing and spinning.

Skim the length of your limbs

                    fluent the rivulets

        rills collide and explode.

River, River, rapturous River

        the pulling, the pulsing,

        I am your prey.

                Your white waters
        seething

    then settling.
Your splashing subsiding,
splendid the run.

We meet the ocean,
its gaze wide horizon.

Oh, to begin your headwaters again.

Waiting at Evening

Sweet limes cling to their dwarf spreading tree.
A wild-eyed dog paces hungry beneath.
I press and lean over this black balcony,
search for you, love, in the street down below.

Sun simmers the sky in pink fading embers.
A zephyr stirs up my long silky robes,
waves of its cool thrilling my limbs,
air everywhere scenting jasmine and rose.

Slender cloud fingers reach across sky,
their star jewels sparkling in violet dusk.
Evening hushes to a deep plaintive humming
and here on my tongue, I taste such longing.

Moody Window

Windows are moody.
Don't ask. They just are.
Protective as overcoats.
Inviting as playgrounds.
Opaque as death.

Last night he left me.
I heard their voices, then slam
of car doors. Our window
went cloudy, refused to allow me
to see who she was.

I tried not to cry,
said I didn't care.
The window cleared up.
More stars than ever,
the night called for a walk.

When I returned tired,
tears dry on my cheek,
I climbed under covers.
The window went cryptic.
And I slept like a prayer.

Into the Mirror

In front of the mirror, she seeks out her self,
looks in past the eyes, the wrinkles of flesh.
Seeing a door, she steps in, but timid.
Who resides there in that room of the self?

Inside a dusky and redolent den
droops an old gentleman, sundials for eyes.
She treads in softly so not to wake him.
Would the artifacts there reveal who she is?

He's stretched out, a plateau in a blanket of mosses
woven in zigzag with verses of rivers.
His arms look like paintbrushes. No, they're just arms
that rest in his lap, the occasional twitch.

On opposite walls, two mirrors face.
One flashes dimly – where she came in?
The gentleman snores, his pencil-hair rattling.
She contemplates him, as she might a child.

Inhabiting earth for eons and eons,
he dreams now of horses he once painted in caves.
Forgetting before, he quickens in infants,
wide-eyed with wonder, enters each breathing life.

The cup by his side holds elixirs of love.
Scribbled nearby lies a bold script for peace.
He seems content. That's the strange dress of sleep.
But when he's awake, the sun burns in his eyes.

He's far from finished, just wait till he's rested.
There are ages to travel before his last sleep
and a peck of perplexes still to stir up.
As she closes the door, does he open an eye?

After Hearing Sylvia Plath Read "Tulips"

*I didn't want any flowers, I only wanted / To lie with my hands turned up
and be utterly empty*

—Sylvia Plath, "Tulips" from *Ariel*

This day is loathe to start, it's gray,
a dreary sky, blunt pencil stub.
But start it does, as if by will,
a will that warns of laziness.

The light augments, not broad or bright.
It merely grows, so duty-bound.
We guess at motive of surroundings,
assign a gloss to what we see.

Suppose we move, step into action,
right foot, left foot, gaining distance,
maintain illusion that there's purpose,
hide from eternal emptiness.

Could we change our tone of voice,
put such words next to each other,
look from someone else's eyes,
and so transform these lives we live?

No way to know until we start,
push our boat from shore to sea,
trust wave enough to throw our net,
if lucky later, finding harbor.

The Next Chapter

I have come to the last page
of this chapter. There, before me,
lies vast whiteness, the empty page
before the next leaf of my life.

Terrifying there, that blizzard of zero.
What will be written? I cannot hold
any phrases across that void.
My voice trembles, limbs shake.

I look for belief, an embrace
to trust, to carry me across.
Look! Letterforms appear,
filling with blood, quickening to bone.

Words emerge out of nothing,
shape as hills of sentences,
a new landscape unfolds.
I take a deep breath, say yes, step in.

II. Metal

Attention! Attention!

Train B is stalled on Platform 9.
We can't say yet when it will go.
So sit, enjoy some bread and wine.
Train B is stalled on Platform 9.
The problem's not your fault or mine.
When it's repaired, we'll let you know.
Train B is stalled on Platform 9.
We can't say yet when it will go.

Blue Boy

Blue boy sits like stone beside the water
sinking into reverie, discovering
new joy there at dawn by water's sparkle,
twinkling, twinkling as if stars had fallen.

Drinking in the scene, its mute elixir,
he does not know he'll forget this moment,
plinking pebbles, watching waves flow outward.
Free, but blind to freedom, still he learns it.

Sinews of the Father

Thank heavens the earth
took over the place.
Tendons and leaf bracts
soft melted the walls.

The garage was always
a den of despair,
my workshop, my car work —
no match for his.

His garage was his haven
for muscular work —
rebuilds and repairs
year after year.

Can a son carry on
the father's mark on the world –
that indelible standard,
that heavy inheritance?

After he died,
I abandoned the place,
a bequest to earth,
its insistent sinews.

Of Robert Frost, Redux

There is a little lightning in his eyes / Iron at the mouth. / His brows ride neither too far up nor down. / He is splendid. With a place to stand. / Some glowing in the common blood. / Some specialness within.

—Gwendolyn Brooks

Suppose he is not Robert Frost there
but another who stands where he is,
would he be a poet too? A
likeness lingers in the eye, some little
similarity. At night, a lightning
flash allows our eyes a quick look in,
just light enough to catch his
face, his own glance back to meet our eyes.
On longer gazing in the day, an iron
trace is noticed there, a fervent clenching at
the mouth. What was neglected? The
coat in tatters, who does he feed, mouth after mouth?
Curious, we might dare to ask his
name and risk that crumpling of his brows
after our question, while we wait and ride
the silence. Who has answers? Neither
summer sun or winter moon, both too
removed from cares we carry, far
too locked in cosmic cycles up
beyond our dreaming world. Nor
would they deign to travel down.

What makes one man be not another? He
who knows keeps close the secret, is
guarding well the puzzle splendid.
The poets and the numbers men with
all their learning ignore a
truth. Some answers have a place
in sunlight, easy for our eyes to
see, but some will always further stand.

Unconcerned, most pass on by, while some,
their incandescent minds a-glowing,
examine further, drawn right in

to look beyond our sunlit world, beyond the
push for blunt survival, common
mandate of mortal blood –
how most men live. But some,
have innate specialness,
a gift perhaps, if summoned out from deep within.

Perfect Pitch

Mid-stage he stands, eye on conductor,
in that glow of spotlight above music stand –
beyond him, fainter, the first rows of faces.

Shakes shimmy up from his knees to his chest.
He counts on long practice to settle the flurry,
fills up his lungs, holds diaphragm taut.

Some flash of blue, from a necklace perhaps,
and he's back at the farm, high sky of August,
fatigue in his arms, in the middle of haying.

He stands on the truck bed, tossing the bales,
over and over, perfect pitch with his fork,
tawny stalks gold, that enamel blue sky.

His voice flows liquid, sweet river of sound,
high and on pitch, perfect and ringing.
It holds him, the audience suspended together.

When the pitch fades to finish,
he sees people standing, smiling and clapping,
as if in that field around the hay wagon.

He closes his eyes, drops down his arms,
bows to the ultimate master of music,
of hay, of all things, the creator of joy.

Again, Deer Season

The store of last year's meat is almost gone
and taste of deer meat haunts his dreams at night.
His blood runs quick, his breath picks up apace
but he has changed from years when he was young.
He's not as keen to down a deer for sport.
He would rather watch their stepping by
than shoot to kill the creatures of his home.
Along with them, the woods are his to roam.
Perhaps there'll be one less in this year's count.
Perhaps there'll be the one that got away.
He'll still rise early, dress for cold and wind,
still take his gun and thermos to his stand.
But when the deer pass close enough to shoot,
he'll rest his gun and silent sing for them.
Homeward bound, he'll think how to explain,
and reconcile himself to other food.

Watching the Daytona 500

He sits on his couch. Cars race on TV,
whining, hurtling at high-speed ennui,
playing gray straight-aways of his everyday life.
He hopes for a crash, not for hurt but for drama,
to break up the boredom of so many laps,
so many Sundays that speed into Mondays,
relentless routine, week after week.

No time for drivers to mull over options,
they run on instinct, on wastage of gas.
Split-second timing, nerves taut as tripwires,
they push for position, clip the pit stops.
Another six-pack, back to the sofa,
sink into the couch, sink into a stupor,
until a crash comes in the rush to the finish.

Smoke would be good, smash of cars against fences,
low fenders scraping, kicking up dust.
Let cars collide but let drivers emerge.
He could pull himself too from his bad, breakdown projects,
the failures, the fracas, his dreams smithereens.
He could smile for the camera, look shaken but brave,
unsung dark horse with a well-practiced wave.

Advances

They are amassing the soldiers again.
Clouds gather, sky darkens, birds have gone mute.
Women are wailing, "We're losing our men."
In the far meadow, a lone shepherd's flute.

Clouds gather, sky darkens, birds have gone mute.
Cannons are primed, the bullets are counted.
In the far meadow, a lone shepherd's flute.
Uniforms fitted while big tanks are mounted.

Cannons are primed, the bullets are counted.
Old ones weep softly, remembering war.
Uniforms fitted while big tanks are mounted.
No one dares ask now what fighting is for.

Old ones weep softly, remembering war.
Women are wailing, "We're losing our men."
No one dares ask now what fighting is for.
They are amassing the soldiers again.

War

Climbing over this rubble, I stumble,
      stomach heaving,

all these hands   these legs,

torn,   as if never
      parts of a living, loved person.

What keeps   my head   looking forward?
I am   barely   tethered   together.

The hands, the hands, what can they do now?

Next step I too could   break into bits,
      feet lost in ruins,

        not moving

one step   one step   to some easier place.

I could not meet a live person now.

How would we
      make our mouths   work again?

Red Wind

I came and saw the red wind howl,
the red wind howl, red wind howl.
I came and saw the red wind howl
and I am at its mercy.

The red wind took my breath away,
my breath away, breath away.
The red wind took my breath away
and I can barely tell it.

How will you save me, scorching steel,
scorching steel, scorching steel?
How will you save me, scorching steel
with your Damascus blade?

You cannot fight the wind with sword,
the wind with sword, wind with sword.
You cannot fight the wind with a sword.
Stop. Listen to the message.

Remains

Here comes a body from the front
for her to handle. She stands frozen,
hears her own voice — shaky, faint.
The body's stiff with rigor mortis.

Someone closed the eyes, thank goodness.
Now her turn to empty pockets –
a spoon, a pen, a candy wrapper,
wallet with a single picture.

She used to do the fingerprinting,
if the fingers were intact.
Now she writes down wounds, tattoos,
and marks which body parts are gone,

then into bag and transfer case
for cortège late this afternoon
where she'll stand straight, saluting hard,
then back to work that no one wants.

Lodestar

I long for a lodestar tonight.
What do I find? Sports bars tonight.

The sad ones trundle off to bed,
as cities run streetcars tonight.

Shopkeepers plan for better days.
They sleep and dream of bazaars tonight.

The old men drink to younger days
while women write memoirs tonight.

Wild winds are keening in the trees.
Teal jungles hide jaguars tonight.

Bare rowboats drift downriver slow.
They seek secure sandbars tonight.

I'd settle for a plaintive song –
strummed low on red guitars tonight.

Ewer

Down old crooked streets,
they seek you, throats parched
from equatorial sun.
Inside the blue door, you
wait as respite from blazing
white walls of the village.

They enter and sigh,
relieved to find you,
pull the weight of your water
up to sore, cracking mouths,
spilling your coolness
in burbled rushing to drink.

I would gladly become
that clay vessel of life,
font of refreshment
after unending heat,
after flaming discord,
a sweet, soothing peace.

When the Women Return

Then out come the women, the long unseen women,
out from the walls, blackened windows, dark veils.

Do they run, do they race out into light?
No, they come slowly, unaccustomed to joy.

They come holding hands, their bodies in smiling.
They come holding close their dreams from deep night.

Above them, the seraphim gather in blessing.
Below them, the land awaits their treading.

A perfume of peace wafts faint through the air,
full of forgiveness, and a scent of blood orange.

III. Fiber

Torso

I meet myself,
a rose clay torso
eleven thousand years old,
open-ended bud of woman,
swell of breast, newborn hips.

I back away from childhood,
peer into the emerald glade,
walk a new walk,
luxurious sway, legs thrust
into unknown territory.

I raise my arms, spiral them up
to a crinkled sky. A shiver stirs
an unfamiliar wanting.
Torn from safe to brazen, my fingers
dance out, tracing fragrances in sultry air.

I scan my body – shoulders, heels.
Who am I now? This long-legged body
I barely noticed in the hollow
under our cliff, glimmers
like dew in morning sun.

I turn, cry out, a lower voice.
A stream of sounds
strange to my hearing,
like leafy vines that girdle my waist,
invites me into the primal line.

Gui: The Chinese Character for Tortoise

Pour water from the pot to well of stone,
then dip the ink stick into water's pool.
Grind the ink, then blacken brush till wet.
It's sixteen strokes, beginning with the head.

Now twirl the brush – the hairs meet at a point.
Place paper so, and hold the brush at slant.
The white page draws the inky brush to it.
And now to make each careful stroke just right.

From black on white, a tortoise starts to form.
First stroke looks good, one more will make the head,
then carapace to right, the feet to left.
One tail stroke, and the symbol is complete.

A tortoise turning sideways, head to north,
she climbs a mountain reaching to the heavens.
That's where she goes to look out to the future,
and carry signs to mortals back on earth.

I ask you, Tortoise: Will my life be long?
Will it be filled with sorrow or with joy?
Please teach me, as I learn to write your name,
when I should show my shell, or softer side.

Two Voices

After Richard Wilbur

Pencil

I have a noble purpose,
brought to a sculpted point,
scribbling song or story,
when our work is joined.
Without your willing surface,
my finest words are null.
Alone, I'm but a painted stick,
my being dull, so dull.

Paper

My task's to bear the beauty
that moves affairs of folk,
receiving wondrous words,
and all they might evoke.
But flat, untouched, and empty
without you, bright utensil,
I'm but a bit of tree brought low,
until I meet you, pencil.

Girl Playing the Cards

I shuffle the cards, again and again.
I want an eight to give me its magic.
Spades or clubs, the suit doesn't matter.
I do the deal but never an eight.

It's ten of diamonds; I wanted an eight.
Eight is infinity sideways beside me.
Now I am eight. Next year I'll be nine.
There is no magic in diamonds, or ten.

If I fall asleep, let the sun warm my face
in whatever light remains in the day,
I'll drift off, dream the magic I look for.
Lady Eight will visit with her wand and a kiss.

Evelyn Snake Woman

Hearing the call of a loon last night, I go visit Evelyn. Older
than I am, she has a musty cabin at the edge of the woods, away
from chattering campers by the lake. She keeps snakes in
cardboard boxes on rough-hewn shelves. Window open, door
unlocked, she is working something in wood with a knife.

She looks up, nods hello. Evelyn has long, black hair tied loosely
in braids. Her clothes are layers of moss green and humus brown,
smelling of pine. Evelyn picks up one of the snakes – color of sand
with muddy diamond patches, as quiet as she is. I ask if the snakes
have names. "No, names are for us, not for these people."

She loops the snake around her neck, sidewinds out the door.
The snake's slow sinuous movements are scary but seductive.
Evelyn is not as graceful. Large and clumsy, she still moves
easily on the breeze through the woods. Campers whisper
her tribe hails from a distant lake in this Canadian wilderness.

Evelyn, snake around her neck, and I walk quietly for hours,
perch on a boulder, walk again. We scan the sky between
tall trees, discover new mushrooms and animal tracks among
the fallen pine needles, listen. We say almost nothing and
the day passes – my first lesson in the largesse of silence.

Tanis

The light has enveloped her,
taken her in
to its delicate story.

She stands, full of girlhood,
for the first time sees
her own wondrous hand.

It is her, it is hers
yet apart from her too,
distant now from her seeing eye.

Yellow grasses, white flowers,
blue trees, and herself
float in this blazing moment of light.

Already her legs are restless to move.
Already the door will ask her to choose.
Already she's older. The light will diminish.

Stop. See her now – how she draws away
from all that she gazes at,
innocence fading with afternoon sun.

The Saga of the Sister from Seilebost

At the left, she stands awkward,
      gusting crooked and sly.
Her pale legs and neck seem to fly from each other.

You mistake her meekness,
      the kid lurks in anger–
Thursday's child, crawling smile, skirt dregs and dirt freckled.

Offer cake, and instead
      she bonds strangely with eggs.
Their skill at beginnings casts her cunning to right.

A glittering prospect
      starts unknotting tangles.
Still muggy of mind, she's unfogging her windows.

Roar of the Girl in the Room

I am the wind, the festering wind,
not camping here where I began as a breeze.

I'll blow out to mountains, the dark, curdling mountains,
bend towards the city, scare down its canyons.

Maybe they'll curse me, they will not tame me.
I'll cripple their lines, their towers that trample.

I'll howl at their prayers. Nothing will stop me.
Don't try to tempt me with reason or love.

If I should tire at playing the tyrant,
I may come home, if ever I find one.

But the walls must be music
or I'll flee with the night.

The Moments Before This One

The shine of her kimono
answers to the light
from the window.

The folds and their shadows
edge out from darkness,
abandon their secrets.

She lifts up the vase,
green as deep seas,
beholding its form.

Her attention expands
to fill this moment.
There is nothing else.

In the next moment,
she will carry the vase,
we don't know where.

For now, she stops
exalted by light
and all the light offers.

We also stop,
see what the light sees,
while everything waits.

Sequins

In secret, she digs back into her past
and finds the shoes that danced in better days.
Saved, they look as grand as she remembered
despite the dust, the years, the joyless haze.

The silver sequins sparkle still a little,
those tiny sequins meant for stepping out.
She dons the shoes. They fit like Cinderella's
and, for a moment, turn her life about.

Back then, she never recognized their magic.
They sparkled, yes, but she had sparkled more.
Now since he'd torn her life, their life, to shreds,
the sequins dazzle, rouse her smothered core.

A noise downstairs, her reverie is shattered.
The sequins are consigned back to the dark.
His drunken steps come angry up the stairs.
Again, his dreaded fists will leave their mark.

Baroque Con Brio

She hunkers down in the high-ceilinged hall,
    tunes her vowels to a ritual keening,
        consonants waiting their turn in the wings.

Bass temblors rise from fissures beneath,
    trace silk brocades through century carpet,
        ride musky currents up gilded walls.

She readies herself to be measured and calm,
    instead falls deep into fogs of forgetting,
        gone her tribe, their welcome, their warnings.

She opens her ear to pulsings of silence.
    Listening doors turn slowly inward,
        walls hold taut, windows go wavy.

Notes collide, wrench apart, and scream.
    She throws her head back, voice leaps on its own,
        crackles and bends her, contorting and aching.

What is she now – furious sound,
    ripping out rules, the room barely stands.
        Corners go haywire, doors pitch forward, back.

The hall twitches tremolo, cannot contain.
  Roof goes riot, squalling clouds run the sky.
  Embryos vibrate, spin out new worlds.

Flutters, trills, and it's over, for now.
  She's spent, thrown down,
    the hall still quivering…

The Necessity of Wilderness

Her wish: To make her garden sing
with words in sweet variety,
plant rows to make the stanzas ring
in rhymed society.

She let the fierce woods stay untrod,
and tended but her humble tract,
turned phrases bright as goldenrod,
left wilderness intact.

And yet the roots spread wide to find
wild roots that grew beyond her fence,
and, that to augment song, inclined
to grant her garden sense.

Violet Edges

What I did not say
was how lovely you looked,
haunting, gazing out the car window.
Your doleful look, I have seen it before.

Who can know the fathoms of grief,
your face flushed gold in late afternoon sun.
It was that tinge, violet at edges,
that drew me in.

As I waved to you,
I waved to myself
saying goodbye to some story of mine
I could barely remember.

Two women, bonded and parting –
you with your sad life yet to walk through,
me writing of melancholy as if by so doing
I could stay its hand.

Plaid

Suppose, just suppose, a bird could leave contrails –
those white streamings of clouds that airplanes make.
Suppose that instead a bird left its color –
a ghost image, threads of its feathers in flight.

A pale-bellied hawk would leave a white band.
A low-flying vulture, a wide swath of black.
The purple of martins would contribute that hue.
White, black, and purple, blue background of sky.

Then just imagine crossing this warp,
other birds wefting their own added colors –
buff hue of mourning doves, two side-by-side,
parallel lines of their soft cooing shades.

A splash from the pond, a mallard takes off,
shiny head of green feathers streaks through the fabric.
A red line of cardinal could add to the pattern.
Cross-weavings create an avian tartan.

The colors would vanish as vapor trails do,
but if lasting enough for our eyes to see them,
what wonder of plaid might we witness in sky
if, instead of cast down, we sometimes looked up.

Oksana Says Goodbye

My handgrip loosens on the metal bar.
My reflexes have slowed. It's time to quit.
Lucky me, no big catastrophes.
But acrobats can't twist and fly forever.

It's tricky to know the best time to retire.
My health is good but eyesight's getting worse.
One needs the vision of a hungry Strix
to see the wires when tent lights go to dim.

I'll miss my slinky, sequined costumes
and when the people gasp – one huge breath.
After such spectacular creations,
I wonder where I'll hear applause again.

The hotel life I gladly leave to others.
That lost its appeal decades ago,
exciting when I was an eager girl
showing off, the spotlight bright and warm.

My daughter will not take up the trapeze.
She'll choose a safer way to live, I hope.
But what a thrill it was each time the men
would swing through air, like birds, to grab me tight –

the pumping beat, the contact, and release,
the beauty of our bodies in their joy.
What thrills the audience felt could never match
the ecstasy of soaring at the heights.

Moon Flight

The moon is full, the deep road is calling.
She rises from dream, drifts out to her car –
her version of steed, intrepid steed.
She guides it west to that great coastal road.
The road now lies empty. The sea rises full,
lapping and lapping the blond sunset beach –
the slips and the shadows, their flit silver shinings,
the endless sea seething, that seeking of shore.

There is no hurry, no trace of insistence.
Time drops out of time, such sweet forgettings.
She's curving south now, rounding the cliffs,
the precipice steep, loud and so close.
Wisps of cloud float on a sly southern wind.
Then up she lifts, lifts higher, and banks.
Updrafts are shifting, cool rivers of air.
The wind has its way, wings dip and soar.

She swoops on a current down towards the coast.
That stark edge of land is still far beneath,
rocks sheeny wet with incessant sea spray.
The battering sea leaps purple and foaming.
From high, her hawk eye traces the strand –
moon-sparkled water colliding with earth.

Fast it all passes under outstretch of wings.
A fresh current catches, she soars toward the moon.

Only the wind at this rarefied height,
all the earth's roarings are distant and mute.
Eucalyptus and redwoods angle down canyons.
A sooty haze wafts towards the cypress at shore.
On a cliff stands a structure, stones piled high,
an odd sentry tower attending the sea.
A single light burns, a candle perhaps,
gives shape to a window, a beacon in blackness.

She circles earthward to spy it up close,
cocks her head, sees a man who sits near the light.
His head is down as he writes at a table.
Night hunkers silent, faint scent of bay.
His eye is drawn to her circling above.
He stands, walks out to the edge of the cliff,
white shirt glowing blue in the soft of the moon.
She lets the breeze carry her down towards the man.

He's watching, keeps turning to keep her in sight.
So they are two – slow spinning creatures,
as the earth moans through the arc of the night.

The bird calls, the man mumbles, regarding each other.
Now she is weary, scans for somewhere to land.
Why not that singular tower of stone?
Her red tail splays out, she hovers, then lands.
Both feet touch down, the sure smack of matter.

After the Fact of Life

They dressed her for death,
big clothing bunched up
around her small frame,
a silk scarf of colors
encircling her neck,
white hair swept taut,
unlike that in life.
She is long gone though,
no trace of her here.
Her ever-sharp eye,
razor-like tongue,
where are they now?
What did she carry
of life into death –
her tilt at injustice,
her constant corrections,
the unstoppable strain
to set all aright?
Does she now inhabit
a mellower mien
with a face of forgiveness,
disposed towards love?
Or is she even fiercer,
avenging angel
learning the sword
of what we might call fate?

As Women Sang, Crickets Would Pause

The women kept singing,
nine ages of them, down by the river.

Yes, there were men, big-hearted men,
and other men.

The women had babies, one after another,
bloody and bawling. The babies grew up.

The women kept singing. Hips played
as they slammed wet clothes against rocks.

The women sang blue, the women sang yellow.
The women sang fancy, the women sang plain.

In fields and in jungles. Before paper and after.
They sang even when all the stars had gone out.

IV. Rock

Inheritance

When it was resolved where the children would live,
which keepsakes and teaspoons would exit with whom,
the parties slunk off in the ashes of wonder
to bad-tempered kitchens and re-built routines
mouthing the mantra: *Call this an adventure.*
Whatever happens to tears not wept?
Do they gather and churn in underground pools,
feeding channels that urge in the dark?
Young ones will grow, find their own mates,
travel in landscapes of scars and mirages.
They will look up thinking they are immune,
till one day they see that they trace the same patterns,
climb trick Escher stairs that instead take them down
where they catch a glimpse of those roiling canals,
unstoppable tides unsteadying their feet.

Two Pages Together

Such emerald greens,
rich reds, royal blues
in the storybook Bible.
Then that one scary picture.
I knew where it was,
each time would skip over it,
turn two pages together
not to see the dark chamber
with windowless walls,
figures leaning and wailing.
More grimacing figures
leaned down through a hole,
a square hole in the ceiling,
their skeletal arms
stretched down in need,
the tumult of bodies
in ragged affliction.
A child would want
no part of that scene.

Now it's your suffering
I want to make vanish,
cast out your torment
from that shuttered room,

fetid with hurt,
you sleeping away
from your torn apart world.
You cannot move
to whatever is next.
I would open a window,
invite in fresh air,
turn two pages together
to banish this picture –
you in that pit,
so deep and so tangled
my arms extended to you
cannot reach.

Fleeting

With what do we contend as much as time?
Endeavors made by day must face the night.
I witness signs of aging past my prime;
the mirror now insists my hair's gone white.
These trees outside my window lose their leaves
that fall to ground where once the neighbor's herd
would wander in from autumn's fields of sheaves.
The cows were sold. Now earth wears winter's beard.
The seasons pass in marching months that make
their journey with no choice except to go.
You too, sweet boy, whom time will not forsake,
while I enjoy your ages as you grow,
will face your own decline with no defence.
But let that time hold off for long years hence.

The Twelfth Hour

It is not the last straw that broke the sad camel's back.
It is the first one – whispering and promising us
       those comfortable futures,
barely noticed breath, weighed with darkness and dream.
       That is the one –
unwitting dawn, crafty with damage, sweet suckling notes
       of a seductive demise.
Is not our fierce birth cry wailing for its inevitable last sigh?

So now pick up the chain, your own link in the line.
Yes, it is heavy, as heavy as years,
       and noisy with remembrance.
What else would you do, but join and carry? Join and carry.
See how the sleek metal glints and dazzles,
       curves catching the light.
You could call it beauty. It's what you have. It is all
that you have, at least for now, if your eyes can see.

When you leave the line, send in the others, waiting their turn.
Gather up their hems dragging behind. Place your hands
       close to theirs,
your kind fingers soothing. They may turn, glance backward
       in your direction.
Sure, go ahead, smile if you wish to. They will not remember
when the first terrors come, when hard links sink them in mud,
but some hint of your scent will be enough to buoy them.

All Souls' Night

After William Butler Yeats and May Sarton

This night the veil is thin. We sense the dread.
They gather, pour their voices into air –
intoxicating fervor of the dead.

"Listen," one voice sounds. "Do not despair.
This realm is not all dreadful. You could learn
from dead souls, essences of love, who care

for you the living. We would rise from urn
and ash, address you as the gods did then,
when people heeded gods. This night we burn

to utter words intended for your pen."
Another voice says, "Aim for nobler views.
This night at threshold lands of ghosts and men,

you seek the more uncanny things let loose,
then run away. You're drawn, repulsed, the thrill
of tempting your demise and so produce

the eerie sights, horrific sounds, the chill."
The voice says, "Such effects are nothing. Raise
your glass to spirit. Ponder how the will,

the soul, desire to live in the next phase,
returning just this night by these gateways."

Rough Coat of Blue

Alone, what now? What can you do?
The dishes? No, you just gaze through
the window out to the shed where he'd
bring in the sheep for their late feed,
then lumber home through dusk to you.

Unwanted future, bleak, askew.
Which path, what first step? Not a clue.
Night looms so dark, fields gone to weed.
Alone, what now?

The loneliness, rough coat of blue,
that wraps around. A residue
of tears overwhelms – grief's sorry creed.
Small boat on ocean, tossed by need,
you hear him breathing. No, not true.
Alone, what now?

Mountain

Mountain, I see you, tall and far from here where
gazing, I call you. Dawn creates your peaks and shadows.
Evening, you're wine-hued. Blue-black stormy clouds
      or white mist,
still you stand steady.

Mountain, I call you, wishing, aching, weather
surging between us. What is it that holds me captive
far across miles? I hear your caves. Your tremble music
beckons me to you.

Mountain, I want you, cryptic, somber substance.
I turn away, you still remain, beguiling presence –
elegant form, your lines, your height, your fervent urging,
high to the heavens.

Riddle that I don't understand, I'm helpless.
Drawn to your wildness, I keep seeking. Then what? Nothing
else can I do but yield in thanks to gifts you grant while
I cry my longing.

The House at the End of the World

We had thought of the house as our house alone,
until one by one all the others arrived.
They trudged up the hill abandoning cars –
derelict, useless – somewhere on the way.
First we welcomed our friends
then all the strangers, nowhere else to go.
A wind grayed the mountaintop
stirred by throngs trundling up,
then swooping below them as if a nudge
for the last steps of their climb.

This decrepit house of bug-eaten wood,
borrows its time from the dark earth beneath.
Ground floor pushes downward, top floor pulls to sky,
windows allow for far views across ranges.
The early arrivers were grudging to later ones,
reluctant to give up what corners they'd claimed.
Men gathered outside around drum barrels of fire,
shifting on feet as they widened the huddles.
The sky thick and heavy turned dark red and restless,
diagonal clouds, hush settling in soil.

Too many now to make introductions,
some do converse, most stay wordless and wary.
A few brought belongings, no one brought cameras.
Children wander through rooms, gaze at grownups for clues.

What must we do while we wait for the end?
No one, not one asks the question aloud.
The house stands silhouetted against deep growling skies.
The hills around pile on top of each other.
No one knows if the prediction will happen
but all muster hope for a livable ending.

When I Ask Why

You say that fire and ice
scream there together.
You say the needle makes
of flesh a garden.
You say that when it stops,
skin shimmies free,
dark gates swing open,
music spills out welcome.
You say the blue-inked picture
can persuade, despite the pain,
that beauty, even bliss,
are within reach.

A Humble Shift of Mind

When I cannot escape the ravages
of earth and my own vagaries of mind,
when I am caught between the wreckages,
we all have wrought, more mean, alas, than kind,
and see what good could be but what exists,
I take myself away to be alone
to where the old oak quietly persists
and music seems to hum within the bone.
This simple unassuming gesture keeps
a reassuring, balanced, even keel.
The problems are not solved, the earth still weeps
but something shifts, the lightness that I feel
allows the play of joy to bless the deed,
to make amends, at least to plant a seed.

The Endless Climb

We struggled up the cliff, the crumbling rock,
clawing hands on edge to find a grip.
The red rock underfoot of such loose stock
would only need the lightest touch to rip.
By cautious steps in order not to trip,
our progress slow, we pushed, exhausted, spent,
and stopped where safe to pause, no backward slip,
daydreaming of a night's rest in our tent
while trying not to question what this venture meant.

Our rucksacks, tightly strapped onto our backs,
their weight, so light at first, felt massive now.
We'd long ceased glancing back to see our tracks –
so far to go, if fates would but allow.
We gave up wiping constant sweat from brow
and tried to keep attention on our goal,
committed to the challenge, to our vow.
We strained our bodies, fought to keep control,
rebellious muscle, wayward mind, and cryptic soul.

The sun now dropping low made shadows deep.
We searched for safe recesses for some rest.
Our aching backs complained, demanded sleep.
At last, we turned to gaze out towards the west.

A mist beneath approached, a phantom guest.
Our campfire offered warmth in evening's chill.
The view, a feast, was sunset's radiant best,
and when we ate, revived, we felt less ill.
The climb so far achieved, we basked in warm goodwill.

Tomorrow would we summit as we'd planned,
then start back down, a quicker step to base?
Nestled between rocks, our sleepy band
was lullabied by stars – a touch of grace.
Not fighting rock, instead we felt embraced
by earth. We thanked our whole surround.
No mishap, no disaster showed its face.
Instead we felt renewed, a peace profound,
as light and free as air, and sure as solid ground.

Evensong

The deep of earth pulls all else down to it –
new roots of spring, the weight of winter's cold.
When weary of air's lightness, all submit –

dawn's promise bright, the night's mystique moonlit.
Great mountains rise, fall back to the hub's strong hold.
The deep of earth pulls all else down to it.

What's born and grows will waste away and quit.
The young and new, in time, become the old.
Then weary of air's lightness, all submit.

That death is sure we hate so to admit,
as if we could dissuade what's been foretold.
The deep of earth pulls all else down to it.

We do the best that living will permit,
each mining that which each considers gold,
then weary of air's lightness, all submit.

To work, to love, we're happy to commit
until what's next, the details yet untold.
The deep of earth pulls all else down to it.
And weary of air's lightness, all submit.

Cord

Black cord stretches from me into earth.
A cord black as onyx winds down past flame
to that underground place.
I know it moves with me, awake and asleep,
even as I ask, Why was I born?
I hear it shriek. I feel it tremble.
I never speak a word of the cord.
The cord says:
Fly through dark night from here to nowhere.
Alarm! Alarm! Cord tears, baby flies.
War, musket, clang of metal in dark.
Blood rises, cord torn, cord torn, blood spills.
Mother cries, "No! No! Come, don't go!
Where are you going? Where have you gone?
You, your voice, I heard before you were born.
I sang to you then, I called your name.
You came in a dream, your face full of blood.
You would not look at me. You cried:

'Don't look at me. Don't learn my face.
I am your body, your child, yourself
but you will not have me, you will not know me,
you will not meet me now.
You will search in the streets, you will search in the faces.

You will search in forests and caverns, their paintings.
You will search way back, search for me in prayers.
You will search in your waking and sleeping and dreaming.
You will search in your mother, and search in your father.
You will search crying in crimson dawns.
I will have abandoned you long at my birth.
Your tears will not pull me. Your shrieks will not find me.
When you call with coyotes, it will not lure me back.
Play, play your flute but play not for me.
I am gone from the blood, the sinew, the bone.
I am gone far and I am gone long.
Hear me out now; you will not hear me again.
Mornings will come and nights rent with longing.
The sorrow will always rest there beside you.
You will forget me. But I will be in the sorrow,
and always, always deep in the earth.
Follow the cord, when you are called.
Follow the cord, when you are ready.
I am the cord. I will carry you home.'"

How to Be an Enigma

Be some other sex.
Speak mandolin.

Pretend you're a taproot.
Soothe bogeymen.

Hang out with big trees –
the baobab, oak.

Let puppets manage you.
Resemble smoke.

Fuel up with lightning.
Cakewalk down stairs.

Drink tea of koan.
Swoon anywhere.

Wrestle with demons,
hide it from your face.

Have asymmetry dress you.
Come from some other place.

Correspond
with the yet-to-be-born.

Spend time with tortoises.
Tolerate scorn.

Visit from some other era.
Don't age.

Travel through mirrors.
Keep off the stage.

Swim in old sepia.
Befriend local spiders.

Practice legerdemain.
Make bramble cider.

Wear clouds to bed.
Suggest solitude.

Light tapers, eat capers.
Sell no thing. Play the oud.

Mala Aria

no sound
except what molecules make
as they leave her spent body
raspy and spreading
poisoning the air

she cannot move
sends instructions to act, synapse by synapse,
from her brain to her arm
Rise up! Rise up!
arm lies mute on the bed

oblivion white
sheets hushed and sweaty
she swims in delirium, soft and seductive
where chill waves of fever
muffle her life

a roaring begins, what dying sounds like
ripples of a tunnel tighten around her
a pinprick of light, it's distant but draws her
breathing in spasms
in a flash she lets go

flung, she is jettisoned out into light
now it's all music, utter perfection
days pass, maybe weeks
down there her body – comatose, quiet –
pulls her back in

jagged, this world
jagged, with edges
jagged, where each feuds with the next
a longing swells up for that other realm
some voice says, Stay, stay there for now

The Rubble Women

After Eleanor Wilner

They gather the detritus
of mistaken dreams,
of lives gone sour,
melodies mislaid.
They stash the mishmash in bags and barrels,
lumber down alleys and wide open roads
weighed down, you would think,
by the loads. But the burden of sorrows
is not their own. They only collect it,
let it jostle and settle
in their pockets and packs,
as they travel the years.

When the women find stones
by the wayside to rest on,
they open their satchels,
spread their collections before them.
They smile at mosaics of carmine and mustard,
surprising jumble of song and refrain,
such a rich mix of earth and cloud smells
they could not have designed.
But here at their fingertips,
they delight in their harvest,
then pack it all up, wandering off,
with ample room still in their swags.

Amaranthine Song

i.   The Long Road

I cannot ride the silver road.
I cannot ride the gold.
I will ride the wooden road
until my bones grow old.

And I will draw my one horse back
if he should run too fast
and whistle to the ghosts that follow
as long as I shall last.

For I don't need a fancy carriage
nor wild winds blowing free.
A bright small breeze would be enough
to keep me company.

ii.   Trouble

I look and see the stars fall down.
How could the stars fall down, fall down?
They gather around my tiny feet.
Then we fall further, me with them.

Where are we falling, stars, dear stars?
I feel the wind rush past my face.
Oh, where is ground for us to fall to?
Where is ground to come to rest?

Stars, we cannot fall forever.
When we land, will we not break?
And still we fall, and still the wind.
And still my questions in the night.

iii.   When the Forests Burn

Bring me a needle of mandrake root
and thread of fiddlehead fern,
and I will sew a cloak of tomorrows
to wear when the forests burn.

From a fallen tree, we will fashion a boat
to sail to an unspoiled land
and pray that our craft will float on the waters
as we shove off from the ash-strewn sand.

We'll carry what memories pockets can hold
and remorse for destructive deeds
to start again where we can settle
and plant more peaceful seeds.

If there should be no harbor or land
for us on the other side,
it will be in the fierce and forever sea
where we will sink and abide.

Ebb Tide

Now is the hour of sour fruit and shadows,
late-mongering wishes and rose-tarnished dreams.

Now is the hour for silent forgiveness,
the tinged lisianthus drooping and done.

Now is the hour to receive the night,
resigning regrets to some makeshift receptacle.

No action called for, no answer required,
the hour comes on its own in the comfort of cycles
and ripening things that keep their own time.

Solace

Let the high mountains hold, their massive sureness
keep you as long as these dark moments pain you.
Let the rich pastures feed your heart's deep yearning,
now and forever.

Let the long lanes and byways guide your movement.
I am beside you, touching, listening, always.
Your life is good. Your life is whole and perfect,
now and forever.

When your tears dry, when sobs subside, be tranquil.
Listen to all the music that surrounds you,
river that lifts you, surging towards the ocean,
where I await you.

If these, my words, feel small, the sense is mighty,
large as you can imagine. Think whole worlds, think
systems of stars and planets, cosmic currents,
where I await you.

What is so small are your sweet tears. Arise now,
step into beauty. You are world and wonder,
everything right and beautiful. Remember.
I am here always.

Notes

page 27: "Ocean Fabric" was inspired by a painting with the same name by Nicholas Longenecker of Philadelphia, PA.

page 29: "Hwyl (hū' əl) *n.* an emotional outburst of eloquence (Welsh). Alternatively, 'hwyl' can mean religious fervor, a style of preaching, a communal mood of fun, enthusiasm, the sail of a ship, goodbye, good luck, or, the soul."
From *Mrs. Byrne's Dictionary of Unusual, Obscure, and Preposterous Words*

page 33: "Aqua Glass" began in connection with a painting with the same name by Nicholas Longenecker of Philadelphia, PA.

page 38: "You, Me, and the Trout" was written to Franz Schubert's Piano Quintet in A Major. (The Trout, D. 667)

page 52: "Blue Boy" is written as a Bodacian, a form written in octaves of two quatrains or multiples of eight lines of trochaic pentameter with a first syllable rhyme pattern of *abab bcbc* and no end rhymes.

page 54: "Of Robert Frost, Redux" is a Golden Shovel poem, the form invented by Terrance Hayes to honor the work of Gwendolyn Brooks. The words of her poem "Of Robert Frost" (the epigraph here) become the end words of each line in the poem.

page 72: "Two Voices" responds to Richard Wilbur's "Two Voices in a Meadow."

page 75: "Tanis" was inspired by Daniel Garber's painting *Tanis, 1915.* (Michener Art Museum, Doylestown, Pennsylvania)

page 76: Seilebost is located on the Isle of Harris, Outer Hebrides, Scotland where historically there has been a heavy Nordic influence, so most of the words here have Nordic origins.

page 77: "Roar of the Girl in the Room" was inspired by a photograph by Joseph Koudelka.

page 78: "The Moments Before This One" was inspired by Daniel Garber's painting *The Studio Wall 1914.* (Michener Art Museum, Doylestown, Pennsylvania)

page 88: "Moon Flight" was inspired by the work of Robinson Jeffers.

page 98: "Fleeting" is a bouts-rimé poem using Shakespeare's Sonnet XII.

page 99:"The Twelth Hour." Each line, including the indented portions, has twelve words.

page 100: "All Souls' Night" is after the poems by William Butler Yeats and May Sarton which use the same title.

page 114: "Mala Aria" is the etymological root of malaria, as the disease was originally thought to be caused by bad air rather than by parasites in *Anopheles* mosquitoes.

About the Author

Elizabeth Bodien grew up in the "burned-over" district of western New York State, but now lives near Hawk Mountain, Pennsylvania. She holds degrees in cultural anthropology, consciousness studies, religion, and poetry. She has worked as an instructor of English in Japan, an organic farmer in the coastal mountains of Oregon, a childbirth instructor in West Africa, a Montessori teacher, and a professor of anthropology. Her poems have appeared in *Parabola*, *Cimarron Review*, *Crannóg*, and *Frogpond*, among other publications in the USA, Ireland, Canada, Australia, India and elsewhere. Her collections are the chapbooks: *Plumb Lines* (Plan B Press); *Rough Terrain: Notes of an Undutiful Daughter* (FootHills), about her mother's decline with Alzheimer's; *Endpapers* (Finishing Line); and *I Sing the Undersung* (Local Gems Press). Now she is working on a collection of her trance writings. www.elizabethbodien.com.

www.ingramcontent.com/pod-product-compliance
Lightning Source LLC
Chambersburg PA
CBHW071831090426
42737CB00012B/2224